THE 10 KETOGENIC CLEANSE

INCREASE YOUR METABOLISM AND DETOX WITH THESE DELICIOUS AND FUN IN A FAST 10 DAY MEAL PLAN

DIANA WATSON

DEDICATION

I dedicate this book to my two beautiful children and my loving husband who have been nothing short of being my light and joy throughout the years.

herein.

Additionally, the information in the following pages is intended only for informational purposes and should thus be thought of as universal. As befitting its nature, it is presented without assurance regarding its prolonged validity or interim quality. Trademarks that are mentioned are done without written consent and can in no way be considered an endorsement from the trademark holder.

CONTENTS

VIP Subscriber List

Dear Reader, If you would like to receive latest tips and tricks on cooking, weight-loss, cookbook recipes, upcoming books & promotions, and more, do subscribe to my mailing list in the link below! I will be giving away a free book that you can download right away as well after you subscribe to show my appreciation!

Here's the link: http://bit.do/dianawatson

INTRODUCTION

Hello, dear reader! I am immensely thankful you are interested in improving your health and fitness by utilizing the methods involved in a ketogenic diet. It is my hope that your determination combined with our thorough meal plan and wonderful recipes will give you a jump start toward your fitness goals. You may have opened this book with a question in mind, "What in the world is a ketogenic cleanse, anyway?" Well, we are glad you asked! A ketogenic cleanse is inspired by the methods of a ketogenic diet. A ketogenic diet aims to change your body's metabolic focus from carbohydrate- based to fat-based fuels in order to produce cellular energy. Its aim is to develop healthy eating habits by replacing useless foods with the nutrients and fuel your body actually needs. This book contains further information about ketogenic dieting and a ten day meal plan accompanied by easy recipes. Having access to a meal plan is one of the most effective ways you can stay motivated along your ketogenic diet journey. So put on your apron, grab your greens, and head to the kitchen for some fat burning, healthy living!

CHAPTER 1: KETO BASICS

BENEFITS OF INCREASED METABOLISM

One of the best ways to learn the meaning of a scientific term is to break it down to its roots. When we break down ketogenic, we see it is comprised of two words: keto and genic. Ketones are fat-based molecules that the body breaks down when it is using fat as its energy source. When used as a suffix, "genic" means "causing, forming, or producing." So, we put these terms together, and we have "ketogenic," or simply put, "causing fat burn." Ergo, the theory behind ketogenic dieting is: when a person reduces the amount of sugar and carbohydrates they consume, the body will begin to breakdown fat it already has in stores all over the body. When your body is cashing in on these stores, it is in a ketogenic state, or "ketosis." When your body consumes food, it naturally seeks carbohydrates for the purpose of breaking them down and using them as fuel. Adversely, a ketogenic cleanse trains your body to use fats for energy instead. This is achieved by lowering the amount of ingested carbohydrates and increasing the amount of ingested fats, which in turn boosts your metabolism.

Only recently has a low carb- high-fat diet plan emerged into the public eye. It is a sharp contrast to the traditional dieting style that emphasizes calorie counting. For many years it was overlooked that crash diets neglect the most important aspect of dieting: food is fuel. A diet is not meant to be treated as a once a year go to method in order to shed holiday weight in January. Rather, a diet is a lifestyle; it is a consistent pattern of how individual fuels their body. A ten day ketogenic cleanse is the perfect way to begin forming healthy eating habits that over time become second nature. If you are tired of losing weight just to gain it all back, never fear. We firmly believe that you can accomplish anything you put your mind to, including living a healthy life! You, like hundreds of others, can successfully accomplish a ketogenic cleanse and change the way you see health, fitness, and life along the way. So let's hit the books and get that metabolism working!

BENEFITS OF CLEANSING

In addition to increased metabolism and fat loss, ketogenic cleansing allows your body naturally rid itself of harmful toxins and wasteful substances. In today's modern world, food is overrun and polluted by genetically modified hormones, artificial flavors and coloring, and copious amounts of unnecessary sugars. Ketogenic cleansing eliminates bread, grains, and many other foods that are most affected by today's modern industrialization. Due to the high amount of naturally occurring foods used in a ketogenic cleanse, the body is able to obtain many vitamins and minerals that are not prevalent in a high carb diet. When the body is consuming sufficient amounts of necessary vitamins and minerals, it is able to heal itself and maintain a healthy immune system. Cleansing your body is one of the best ways to achieve, and maintain pristine health.

CHAPTER 2: MEAL PLAN MADNESS

One of the best ways to stay motivated, when dieting, is to find a meal plan that is easy to follow and easy on the budget. Ketogenic meals are designed to be filling while keeping within the perimeters of low-carb, high-fat guidelines. Ideally, you want to aim for 70% fats, 25% protein, and 5% carbohydrates in your diet. As long as the materials you use to build your meals are low in carbs and high in fats, feel free to experiment and find what is right for you. Each and every one of us is different, and that's okay. After all, this meal plan is for YOU!

Below is a ten-day meal plan, designed with a busy schedule in mind, which will not break the bank! All of these meals can be prepared in 30 minutes or less, and many of them are much quicker than that! There is also a list of ingredients for each meal located in the recipe chapter so you can go to the grocery store knowing exactly what you need!

	Breakfast	Lunch	Dinner
Day 1	**California Chicken Omelet** • Fat: 32 grams • 10 minutes to prepare • Protein: 25 grams • 10 minutes of cooking • Net carbs: 4 grams	**Cobb Salad** • Fat: 48 grams • 10 minutes to prepare • Protein: 43 grams • 0 minutes of cooking • Net carbs: 3 grams	**Chicken Peanut Pad Thai** • Fat: 12 grams • 15 minutes to prepare • Protein: 30 grams • 15 minutes of cooking • Net carbs: 2 grams
Day 2	**Easy Blender Pancakes** • Fat: 29 grams • 5	**Sardine Stuffed Avocados** • Fat: 29 grams • 10 minutes to prepare	**Chipotle Fish Tacos** • Fat: 20 grams • 5 minutes to prepare • Protein:

	minutes to prepare • Protein: 41 grams • 10 minutes of cooking • Net carbs: 4 grams	• Protein: 27 grams • 0 minutes of cooking • Net Carbs: 5 grams	24 grams • 15 minutes of cooking • Net carbs: 5 grams
Day 3	**Steak and Eggs** • Fat: 36 grams • 10 minutes to prepare • Protein: 47 grams • 5 minutes of cooking • Net carbs: 3 grams	**Low-Carb Smoothie Bowl** • Fat 35 grams • 5 minutes to prepare • Protein: 20 grams • 0 minutes of cooking • Net carbs: 5 grams	**Avocado Lime Salmon** • Fat: 27 grams • 20 minutes to prepare • Protein: 37 grams • 10 minutes of cooking • Net carbs: 5 grams
KEEP IT UP!!!	During the course of your plan, especially around days 3 and 4, you may begin to feel like you don't have it in you. You may have thoughts telling you that you cannot last for ten days on this type pf cleanse. Do not allow feelings of discouragement bother you because guess what? We all feel that way		

	sometimes! A ketogenic diet causes your body to process energy like it never has before. Keep pressing on! Your body will thank you and so will you!		
Day 4	**Low-Carb Smoothie Bowl** • Fat: 35 grams • 5 minutes to prepare • Protein: 35 grams • 0 minutes of cooking • Net carbs: 4 grams	**Pesto Chicken Salad** • Fat: 27 grams • 5 minutes to prepare • Protein: 27 grams • 10 minutes of cooking • Net carbs: 3 grams	**Sriracha Lime Flank Steak** • Fat: 32 grams • 5 minutes to prepare • Protein: 48 grams • 10 minutes of cooking • Net Carbs: 5 grams
Day 5	**Feta and Pesto Omelet** • Fat: 46 grams • 5 minutes of preparation • Protein: 30 grams • 5 minutes of cooking • Net carbs: 2.5 grams	**Roasted Brussel Sprouts** • Fat: 21 grams • 5 minutes to prepare • Protein: 21 grams • 30 minut	**Low carb Sesame Chicken** • Fat: 36 grams • 15 minutes to prepare • Protein: 41 grams • 15 minut

		es of cooking • Net carbs: 4 grams	es of cooking • Net carbs: 4 grams
Day 6	**Raspberry Cream Crepes** • Fat: 40 grams • 5 minutes of preparation • Net carbs: 8 grams • 15 minutes of cooking • Protein 15 grams	**Shakshuka** • Fat: 34 grams • Protein 35 grams • Net carbs: 4 grams • 10 minutes of preparation • 10 minutes of cooking	**Sausage in a Pan** • Fat: 38 grams • 10 minutes of preparation • Protein: 30 grams • 25 minutes of cooking • Net Carbs: 4 grams
Day 7	**Green Monster Smoothie** • Fat: 25 grams • 5 minutes of preparation • Protein: 30 grams • 0 minutes of cooking • Net Carbs: 3 grams	**Tuna Tartare** • Fat: 24 grams • 15 minutes of preparation • Protein: 56 grams • 0 minutes of	**Pesto Chicken Salad** • Fat: 27 grams • 5 minutes of preparation • Protein: 27 grams • 10 minutes of

		cooking	cooking
		• Net Carbs: 4 grams	• Net carbs: 3 grams
ALMOST THERE !!	By now, you can be certain you are seeing physical results such as reduced body fat and more energy! You are doing a fantastic job, and you only have three days left! Keep up the good work; you owe it to yourself.		
Day 8	**Shakshuka** • Fat: 34 grams • 10 minutes of preparation • Protein 35 grams • 10 minutes of cooking • Net carbs: 4 grams	**Grilled Halloumi Salad** • Fat: 47 grams • 15 minutes of preparation • Protein: 21 grams • 0 minutes of cooking • Net carbs: 2 grams	**Keto Quarter Pounder** • Fat: 34 grams • 10 minutes of preparation • Protein: 25 grams • 8 minutes of cooking • Net carbs: 4 •
Day 9	**Easy Blender Pancakes** • Fat: 29 grams • 5	**Broccoli Bacon Salad** • Fat: 31 grams • 15 minutes of preparation • Protein: 10 grams	**Sardine Stuffed Avocados** • Fat: 29 grams • 10

	minutes of preparation • Protein: 41 grams • 10 minutes of cooking • Net carbs: 4 grams	• 6 minutes of cooking • Net carbs: 5 grams	minutes to prepare • Protein: 27 grams • 0 minutes to cook • Net Carbs: 5 grams
Day 10	**California Chicken Omelet** • Fat 32 grams • 10 minutes to prepare • Protein 25 grams • 10 minutes of cooking • Net Carb: 3 grams	**Shrimp Scampi** • Fat: 21 grams • 5 minutes to prepare • Protein: 21 grams • 30 minutes of cooking • Net carbs: 4 grams	**Tuna Tartare** • Fat: 36 grams • 15 minutes to prepare • Protein: 41 grams • 15 minutes of cooking • Net carbs: 4 grams
YOU DID IT!!	Congratulations! You have successfully completed a 10 day ketogenic cleanse. By now your body has adjusted to its new source of energy, expelled dozens of harmful toxins, and replenished itself with many vitamins and minerals it may have been lacking. Way		

	to go on a job well done!

CHAPTER 3: BREAKFAST IS FOR CHAMPIONS

Breakfast is by far the most important meal of the day for one reason: it set the tone for the rest of your day. In order to hit the ground running, it is vital that one starts each day with foods that fuel an energetic and productive day. This chapter contains ten ketogenic breakfast ideas that will have you burning fat and conquering your day like you never imagined.

1. CALIFORNIA CHICKEN OMELET

- This recipe requires 10 minutes of preparation, 10 minutes of cooking time and serves 1

- Net carbs: 4 grams

- Protein: 25 grams

- Fat : 32 grams

What you will need:

- Mayo (1 tablespoon)

- Mustard (1 teaspoon)

- Campari tomato

- Eggs (2 large beaten)

- Avocado (one-fourth, sliced)

- Bacon (2 slices cooked and chopped)

- Deli chicken (1 ounce)

What to do:

1. Place a skillet on the stove over a burner set to a medium heat and let it warm before adding the eggs and seasoning as needed.

2. Once eggs are cooked about halfway through, add bacon, chicken, avocado, tomato, mayo, and mustard on one side of the eggs.

3. Fold the omelet onto its self, cover and cook for 5 additional minutes.

4. Once eggs are fully cooked, and all ingredients are warm, through the center, your omelet is ready.

5. Bon apatite!

2. STEAK AND EGGS WITH AVOCADO

- This recipe requires 10 minutes of preparation, 5 minutes of cooking time and serves 1
- Net Carbs: 3 grams
- Protein: 44 grams
- Fat: 36 grams

What you will need:

- Salt and pepper
- Avocado (one-fourth, sliced)
- Sirloin steak (4 ounces)
- Eggs (3 large)
- Butter (1 tablespoon)

What to do:

1. Melt the tablespoon of butter in a pan and fry all 3 eggs to the desired doneness. Season the eggs with salt and pepper.

2. In a different pan, cook the sirloin steak to your preferred taste and slice it into thin strips. Season the steak with salt and pepper.

3. Sever your prepared steak and eggs with slices of avocado.

4. Enjoy!

3. PANCAKES IN A BLENDER

- This recipe requires 5 minutes of preparation, 10 minutes of cooking time and serves 1
- Net Carbs: 4 grams
- Protein: 41 grams
- Fat: 29 grams

What you will need:

- Whey protein powder (1 scoop)
- Eggs (2 large)
- Cream cheese (2 ounces)
- Just a pinch of cinnamon and a pinch of salt

What to do:

1. Combine cream cheese, eggs, protein powder, cinnamon, and salt in a blender. Blend for 10 seconds and let stand.
2. While letting batter stand, warm a skillet over medium heat.
3. Pour about ¼ of the batter into warmed skillet and let cook. When bubbles begin to emerge on the surface, flip the pancake.
4. Once flipped, cook for 15 seconds. Repeat until the remainder of the batter is used up.
5. Top with butter and/ or sugar- free maple syrup and you are all set!
6. Chow time!

4. LOW CARB SMOOTHE BOWL

- Net Carbs: 4 grams
- Protein: 35 grams
- Fat: 35 grams
- It takes 5 minutes to prepare and serves 1.

What you will need:

- Spinach (1 cup)

- Almond milk (half a cup)

- Coconut oil (1 tablespoon)

- Low carb protein powder (1 scoop)

- Ice cubes (2 cubes)

- Whipping cream (2 T)

- Optional toppings can include: raspberries, walnuts, shredded coconut, or chia seeds

What to do:

1. Place spinach in the blender. Add almond milk, cream, coconut oil, and ice. Blend until thoroughly and evenly combined.

2. Pour into bowl.

3. Top with toppings or stir lightly into a smoothie.

4. Treat yourself!

5. FETA AND PESTO OMELET

- This recipe requires 5 minutes of preparation, 5 minutes of cooking time and serves 1
- Net Carbs: 2.5 grams
- Protein: 30 grams
- Fat: 46 grams

What you will need:

- Butter (1 tablespoon)
- Eggs (3 large)
- Heavy cream (1 tablespoon)
- Feta cheese (1 ounce)
- Basil pesto (1 teaspoon)
- Tomatoes (optional)

What to do:

1. Heat pan and melt butter.
2. Beat eggs together with heavy whipping cream (will give eggs a fluffy consistency once cooked).
3. Pour eggs into pan and cook until almost done, add feta and pesto to on half of the eggs.

4. Fold omelet and cook for an additional 4-5 minutes.

5. Top with feta and tomatoes, and eat up!

6. CREPES WITH CREAM AND RASPBERRIES

- This recipe requires 5 minutes of preparation, 15 minutes of cooking time and serves 2

- Net Carbs: 8 grams

- Protein: 15 grams

- Fat: 40 grams

What you will need:

- Raspberries (3 ounces, fresh or frozen)

- Whole Milk Ricotta (half a cup and 2 tablespoons)

- Erythritol (2 tablespoons)

- Eggs (2 large)

- Cream Cheese (2 ounces)

- Pinch of salt

- Dash of Cinnamon

- Whipped cream and sugar- free maple syrup to go on top

What to do:

1. In a blender, blend cream cheese, eggs, erythritol, salt, and cinnamon for about 20 seconds, or until there are no lumps of cream cheese.

2. Place a pan on a burner turned to a medium heat before coating in cooking spray. Add 20 percent of your batter to the pan in a thin layer. Cook crepe until the underside becomes slightly darkened. Carefully flip the crepe and let the reverse side cook for about 15 seconds.

3. Repeat step 3 until all batter is used.

4. Without stacking the crepes, allow them to cool for a few minutes.

5. After the crepes have cool, place about 2 tablespoons of ricotta cheese in the center of each crepe.

6. Throw in a couple of raspberries and fold the side to the middle.

7. Top those off with some whipped cream and sugar-free maple syrup and...

8. Viola! You're a true chef! Indulge in your creation!

7. GREEN MONSTER SMOOTHIE

- This recipe requires 10 minutes of preparation, 0 minutes of cooking time and serves 1
- Net Carbs: 4 grams
- Protein: 30 grams
- Fat: 25 grams

What you will need:

- Almond milk (one and a half cups)
- Spinach (one-eighth of a cup)
- Cucumber (a fourth of a cup)
- Celery (a fourth of a cup)
- Avocado (a fourth of a cup)
- Coconut oil (1 tablespoon)
- Stevia (liquid, 10 drops)
- Whey Protein Powder (1 scoop)

What to do:

1. In a blender, blend almond milk and spinach for a few pulses.

2. Add remaining ingredients and blend until

    thoroughly combined.

3. Add optional matcha powder, if desired, and enjoy!

CHAPTER 4: LUNCH CRUNCH

Eating a healthy lunch when you are limited on time due to, work, school, or taking care of your kids can be a tumultuous task. Thankfully, we have compiled a list of eight quick and easy recipes to accompany the ten-day meal plan laid out in chapter 2! Many find it advantageous, especially if you work throughout the week, to prepare your meals ahead of time. Thankfully, these lunch recipes are also easy to pack and take on the go!

1. OFF THE COBB SALAD

- Net carbs: 3 grams
- Protein: 43 grams
- Fat: 48 grams
- It takes 10 minutes to prepare and serves 1.

What you will need:

- Spinach (1 cup)
- Egg (1, hard-boiled)
- Bacon (2 strips)

- Chicken breast (2 ounces)

- Campari tomato (one-half of tomato)

- Avocado (one-fourth, sliced)

- White vinegar (half of a teaspoon)

- Olive oil (1 tablespoon)

What to do:

1. Cook chicken and bacon completely and cut or slice into small pieces.
2. Chop remaining ingredients into bite size pieces.
3. Place all ingredients, including chicken and bacon, in a bowl, toss ingredients in oil and vinegar.
4. Enjoy!

2. AVOCADO AND SARDINES

- Net Carbs: 5 grams

- Protein: 27 grams

- Fat: 52 grams

- It takes 10 minutes to prepare and serves 1.

What you will need:

- Fresh lemon juice (1 tablespoon)

- Spring onion or chives (1 or small bunch)

- Mayonnaise (1 tablespoon)

- Sardines (1 tin, drained)

- Avocado (1 whole, seed removed)

- Turmeric powder (a fourth of a teaspoon) or freshly ground turmeric root (1 teaspoon)

- Salt (a fourth of a teaspoon)

What to do:

1. Begin by cutting the avocado in half and removing its seed.

2. Scoop out about half the avocado and set aside (shown below).

3. In a small bowl, mash drained sardines with a fork.

4. Add onion (or chives), turmeric powder, and mayonnaise. Mix well.

5. Add removed avocado to sardine mixture.

6. Add lemon juice and salt.

7. Scoop the mixture into avocado halves.

8. Dig in!

3. CHICKEN SALAD A LA PESTO

- This recipe requires 5minutes of preparation, 10 minutes of cooking time and serves 4
- Net Carbs: 3 grams
- Protein: 27 grams
- Fat: 27 grams

What you will need:

- Garlic pesto (2 tablespoons)
- Mayonnaise (a fourth of a cup)
- Grape tomatoes (10, halved)
- Avocado (1, cubed)
- Bacon (6 slices, cooked crisp and crumbled)
- Chicken (1 pound, cooked and cubed)
- Romaine lettuce (optional)

What to do:

1. Combine all ingredients in a large mixing bowl.
2. Toss gently to spread mayonnaise and pesto evenly throughout.

3. If desired, wrap in romaine lettuce for a low-carb BLT chicken wrap.

4. Bon apatite!

4. BACON AND ROASTED BRUSSEL SPROUTS

- This recipe requires 5 minutes of preparation, 30 minutes of cooking time and serves 4
- Net Carbs: 4 grams
- Protein: 15 grams
- Fat: 21 grams

What you will need:

- Bacon (8 strips)
- Olive oil (2 tablespoons)
- Brussel sprouts (1 pound, halved)
- Salt and pepper

What to do:

1. Preheat oven to 375 degrees Fahrenheit.
2. Gently mix Brussel sprouts with olive oil, salt, and pepper.
3. Spread Brussel sprouts evenly onto a greased baking sheet.

4. Bake in the oven for 30 minutes. Shake the pan about halfway through to mix the Brussel sprout halves up a bit.

5. While Brussel sprouts are in the oven, fry bacon slices on the stovetop.

6. When bacon is fully cooked, let cool and chop it into bite size pieces.

7. Combine Bacon and Brussel sprouts in a bowl, and you're finished!

8. Feast!!

5. GRILLED HALLOUMI SALAD

- Net Carbs: 7 grams

- Protein: 21 grams

- Fat: 47 grams

- It takes 15 minutes to prepare and serves 1.

What you will need:

- Chopped walnuts (half of an ounce)

- Baby arugula (1 handful)

- Grape tomatoes (5)

- Cucumber (1)

- Halloumi cheese (3 ounces)

- Olive oil (1 teaspoon)

- Balsamic vinegar (half of a teaspoon)

- A pinch of salt

What to do:

1. Slice halloumi cheese into slices 1/3 of an in thick.

2. Grill cheese for 3 to 5 minutes, until you see grill lines, on each side.

3. Wash and cut veggies into bite size pieces, place in salad bowl.

4. Add rinsed baby arugula and walnuts to veggies.

5. Toss in olive oil, balsamic vinegar, and salt.

6. Place grilled halloumi on top of veggies, and your lunch is ready!

7. Eat those greens and get back to work!

6. BACON BROCCOLI SALAD

- This recipe requires 15 minutes of preparation, 6 minutes of cooking time and serves 5.
- Net Carbs: 5 grams
- Protein: 10 grams
- Fat: 31 grams

What you will need:

- Sesame oil (half of a teaspoon)
- Erythritol (1 and a half tablespoons) or stevia to taste
- White vinegar (1 tablespoon)
- Mayonnaise (half of a cup)
- Green onion (three-fourths of an ounce)
- Bacon (a fourth of a pound)
- Broccoli (1 pound, heads, and stalks cut and trimmed)

What to do:

1. Cook bacon and crumble into bits.

2. Cut broccoli into bite sized pieces.

3. Slice scallions.

4. Mix mayonnaise, vinegar, erythritol (or stevia), and sesame oil, to make the dressing.

5. Place broccoli and bacon bits in a bowl and toss with dressing.

6. Viola!

7. TUNA AVOCADO TARTARE

- Net Carbs: 4 grams

- Protein: 56 grams

- Fat: 24 grams

- It takes 15 minutes to prepare and serves 2.

What you will need:

- Sesame seed oil (2 tablespoons)

- Sesame seeds (1 teaspoon)

- Cucumbers (2)

- Lime (half of a whole lime)

- Mayonnaise (1 tablespoon)

- Sriracha (1 tablespoon)

- Olive oil (2 tablespoons)

- Jalapeno (one-half of the whole jalapeno)

- Scallion (3 stalks)

- Avocado (1)

- Tuna steak (1 pound)

- Soy sauce (1 tablespoon)

What to do:

1. Dice tuna and avocado into ¼ inch cubes, place in a bowl.

2. Finely chop scallion and jalapeno, add to bowl.

3. Pour olive oil, sesame oil, sriracha, soy sauce, mayonnaise, and lime into a bowl.

4. Using hands, toss all ingredients to combine evenly. Using a utensil may breakdown avocado, which you want to remain chunky, so it is best to use your hands.

5. Top with sesame seeds and serve with a side of sliced cucumber.

6. There's certainly something fishy about this recipe, but it tastes great! Enjoy!

8. WARM SPINACH AND SHRIMP

- This recipe requires 15 minutes of preparation, 6 minutes of cooking time and serves 5.
- Fat: 24 grams
- Protein: 36 grams
- Net Carbs: 3 grams
- Takes10 minutes to prepare, 5 minutes to cook, and serves 2.

What you will need:

- Spinach (2 handfuls)
- Parmesan (half a tablespoon)
- Heavy cream (1 tablespoon)
- Olive oil (1 tablespoon)
- Butter (2 tablespoons)
- Garlic (3 cloves)
- Onion (one fourth of whole onion)
- Large raw shrimp (about 20)
- Lemon (optional)

What to do:

1. Place peeled shrimp in cold water.

2. Chop onions and garlic into fine pieces.

3. Heat oil in a pan, over medium heat. Cook shrimp in oil until lightly pink (we do not want them fully cooked here). Remove shrimp from oil and set aside.

4. Place chopped onions and garlic into the pan, cook until onions are translucent. Add a dash of salt.

5. Add butter, cream, and parmesan cheese. Stir until you have a smooth sauce.

6. Let the sauce cook for about 2 minutes, so it will thicken slightly.

7. Place shrimp back into the pan and cook until done. This should take no longer than 2 or 3 minutes. Be careful not to overcook the shrimp; it will become dry and tough!

8. Remove shrimp and sauce from pan and replace with spinach. Cook spinach VERY briefly

9. Place warmed spinach onto a plate.

10. Pour shrimp and sauce over a bed of spinach, squeeze some lemon on top, if you like, and you're ready to chow down!

CHAPTER 5: THINNER BY DINNER

It's the end of the day and you are winding down from a hard day's work. Your body does not require a lot of energy while you sleep; therefore, dinner will typically consist of less fat and more protein.

1. CHICKEN PAD THAI

- Net Carbs: 7 grams
- Protein: 30 grams
- Fat: 12 grams
- It takes 15 minutes to prepare, 15 minutes to cook, and serves 4.

What you will need:

- Peanuts (1 ounce)
- Lime (1 whole)
- Soy sauce (2 tablespoons)
- Egg (1 large)
- Zucchini (2 large)
- Chicken thighs (16 ounces, boneless and skinless)

- Garlic (2 cloves, minced)

- White onion (1,chopped)

- Olive oil (1 tablespoon)

- Chili flakes (optional)

What to do:

1. Over medium heat, cook olive oil and onion until translucent. Add the garlic and cook about three minutes (until fragrant).

2. Cook chicken in the pan for 5 to 7 minutes on each side (until fully cooked). Remove chicken from heat and shred it using a couple of forks.

3. Cut ends off zucchini and cut into thin noodles. Set zucchini noodles aside.

4. Next, scramble the egg in the pan.

5. Once the egg is fully cooked, and the zucchini noodles and cook for about 2 minutes.

6. Add the previously shredded chicken to the pan.

7. Give it some zing with soy sauce, lime juice, peanuts, and chili flakes.

8. Time to eat!

2. CHIPOTLE STYLE FISH TACOS

- Fat: 20 grams

- Protein: 24 grams

- Net Carbs: 7 grams

- It takes 5 minutes to prepare, 15 minutes to cook, and serves 4.

What you will need:

- Low carb tortillas (4)

- Haddock fillets (1 pound)

- Mayonnaise (2 tablespoons)

- Butter (2 tablespoons)

- Chipotle peppers in adobo sauce (4 ounces)

- Garlic (2 cloves, pressed)

- Jalapeño (1 fresh, chopped)

- Olive oil (2 tablespoons)

- Yellow onion (half of an onion, diced)

What to do:

1. Fry diced onion (until translucent) in olive oil in a high sided pan, over medium- high heat.

2. Reduce heat to medium, add jalapeno and garlic. Cook while stirring for another two minutes.

3. Chop the chipotle peppers and add them, along with the adobo sauce, to the pan.

4. Add the butter, mayo, and fish fillets to the pan.

5. Cook the fish fully while breaking up the fillets and stirring the fish into other ingredients.

6. Warm tortillas for 2 minutes on each side.

7. Fill tortillas with fishy goodness and eat up!

3. SALMON WITH AVOCADO LIME SAUCE

- Net Carbs: 5 grams

- Protein: 37 grams

- Fat: 27 grams

- It takes 20 minutes to prepare, 10 minutes to cook, and serves 2.

What you will need:

- Salmon (two 6 ounce fillets)
- Avocado (1 large)
- Lime (one-half of a whole lime)
- Red onion (2 tablespoons, diced)
- Cauliflower (100 grams)

What to do:

1. Chop cauliflower in a blender or food processor then cooks it in a lightly oiled pan, while covered,

for 8 minutes. This will make the cauliflower rice-like.

2. Next, blend the avocado with squeezed lime juice in the blender or processor until smooth and creamy.

3. Heat some oil in a skillet and cook salmon (skin side down first) for 4 to 5 minute. Flip the fillets and cook for an additional 4 to 5 minutes.

4. Place salmon fillet on a bed of your cauliflower rice and top with some diced red onion.

4. SIRACHA LIME STEAK

- Net Carbs: 5 grams

- Protein: 48 grams

- Fat: 32 grams

- It takes 5 minutes to prepare, 10 minutes to cook, and serves 2.

What you will need:

- Vinegar (1 teaspoon)
- Olive oil (2 tablespoons)
- Lime (1 whole)
- Sriracha (2 tablespoons)
- Flank steak (16 ounces)
- Salt and pepper

What to do:

1. Season steak, liberally, with salt and pepper. Place on baking sheet, lined with foil, and broil in oven for 5 minutes on each side (add another minute or

two for a well-done steak). Remove from oven, cover, and set aside.

2. Place sriracha in a small bowl and squeeze lime into it. Whisk in salt, pepper, and vinegar.

3. Slowly pour in olive oil.

4. Slice steak into thin slices, slather on your sauce, and enjoy!

5. Feel free to pair this recipe with a side of greens such as asparagus or broccoli.

5. LOW CARB SESAME CHICKEN

- Net Carbs: 4 grams
- Protein: 45 grams
- Fat: 36 grams
- Takes 15minutes to prepare, 15 minutes to cook, and serves 2.

What you will need:

- Broccoli (three-fourths of a cup, cut bite size)
- Xanthan gum (a fourth of a teaspoon)
- Sesame seeds (2 tablespoons)

- Garlic (1 clove)

- Ginger (1 cm cube)

- Vinegar (1 tablespoon)

- Brown sugar alternative (Sukrin Gold is a good one) (2 tablespoons)

- Soy sauce (2 tablespoons)

- Toasted sesame seed oil (2 tablespoons)

- Arrowroot powder or cornstarch (1 tablespoon)

- Chicken thighs (1poundcut into bite sized pieces)

- Egg (1 large)

- Salt and pepper

- Chives (optional)

What to do:

1. First, we will make the batter by combining the egg with a tablespoon of arrowroot powder (or cornstarch). Whisk well.

2. Place chicken pieces in batter. Be sure to coat all sides of chicken pieces with the batter.

3. Heat one tablespoon of sesame oil, in a large pan. Add chicken pieces to hot oil and fry. Be gentle

when flipping the chicken, you want to keep the batter from falling off. It should take about 10 minutes for them to cook fully.

4. Next, make the sesame sauce. In a small bowl, combine soy sauce, brown sugar alternative, vinegar, ginger, garlic, sesame seeds, and the remaining tablespoon of toasted sesame seed oil. Whisk very well.

5. Once the chicken is fully cooked, add broccoli and the sesame sauce to the pan and cook for an additional 5 minutes.

6. Spoon desired amount into a bowl, top it off with some chopped chives, and relish in some fine dining at home!

6. PAN 'O SAUSAGE

- Net Carbs: 4 grams

- Protein: 30 grams

- Fat: 38 grams

- It takes 10 minutes to prepare, 25 minutes to cook, and serves 2.

What you will need:

- Basil (half a teaspoon)

- Oregano (half a teaspoon)

- White onion (1 tablespoon)

- Shredded mozzarella (a fourth of a cup)

- Parmesan cheese (a fourth of a cup)

- Vodka sauce (half a cup)

- Mushrooms (4 ounces)

- Sausage (3 links)

- Salt (a fourth of a teaspoon)

- Red pepper (a fourth of a teaspoon, ground)

What to do:

1. Preheat oven to 350 degrees Fahrenheit.

2. Heat an iron skillet over medium flame. When skillet is hot, cook sausage links until almost thoroughly cooked.

3. While sausage is cooking, slice mushrooms and onion.

4. When sausage is almost fully cooked, remove links from heat and place mushrooms and onions in skillet until brown.

5. Cut sausage into pieces about ½ inch thick and place pieces in the pan.

6. Season skillet contents with oregano, basil, salt, and red pepper.

7. Add vodka sauce and parmesan cheese. Stir everything together.

8. Place skillet in oven for 15 minutes. Sprinkle mozzarella on top a couple minutes before removing the dish from oven.

9. Once 15 minutes is up, remove skillet from the oven and let cool for a few minutes.

10. Dinner time!

7. QUARTER POUNDER KETO BURGER

- Net Carbs: 4 grams

- Protein: 25 grams

- Fat: 34 grams

- Takes 10 minutes to prepare, 8 minutes to cook, and serves 2.

What you will need:

- Basil (half a teaspoon)
- Cayenne (fourth a teaspoon)
- Crushed red pepper (half a teaspoon)
- Salt (half a teaspoon)
- Lettuce (2 large leaves)
- Butter (2 tablespoons)
- Egg (1 large)
- Sriracha (1 tablespoon)
- Onion (fourth of whole onion)
- Plum tomato (half of the whole tomato)

- Mayo (1 tablespoon)

- Pickled jalapenos (1 tablespoon, sliced)

- Bacon (1 strip)

- Ground beef (half a pound)

- Bacon (1 strip)

What to do:

1. Knead mean for about three minutes.

2. Chop bacon, jalapeno, tomato, and onion into fine pieces. (shown below)

3. Knead in mayo, sriracha, egg, and chopped ingredients, and spices into the meat.

4. Separate meat into four even pieces and flatten them (not thinly, just press on the tops to create a flat surface). Place a tablespoon of butter on top of two of the meat pieces. Take the pieces that do not have butter in them and set them on top of the buttered ones (basically creating a butter and meat sandwich). Seal the sides together, concealing the butter within.

5. Throw the patties on the grill (or in a pan) for about 5 minutes on each side. Caramelize some onions if you want too!

6. Prepare large leaves of lettuce by spreading some mayo onto them. Once patties are finished, place them on one-half of the lettuce, add your desired burger toppings, and fold the other half over of the lettuce leaf over the patty.

7. Burger time!

...

...

BREAKFAST

BREAKFAST RECIPES TO START YOUR DAY STRONG

Sconey Sconey Sunday - 6 SmartPoints Per Serving

This breakfast dish is best made on the weekend and enjoyed all week long. This breakfast should be filling in the moment due to the fluffiness of the scone and should keep you satisfied all morning because of the liberal use of peaches. If you are new to baking, or just a little bit afraid of your own oven, this is a great recipe to start with. There is no need to wait for any ingredients to rise and it builds the foundation for many other scone recipes. You can replace the peach with blueberries, banana, apple, etc. Try and experiment to find what you like most.

Ready in 25 Minutes

10 minutes to prep and 15 minutes to cook

Ingredients (serves 4):

2/3 cups of all purpose flour

½ teaspoon of baking powder

½ teaspoon of baking soda

1 teaspoon of powdered sugar

2 tablespoons of sugar

½ teaspoon of half and half

1 teaspoon of margarine

1/3 cup of vanilla yogurt (I highly recommend Stoneyfield for the best results)

1 teaspoon of salt

3 tablespoons of chopped peaches (if you are using canned peaches, make sure you drain the peaches and give the peaches some time to dry. I recommend not using canned as they tend to contain additional sugars that add unnecessary calories and distort the flavor of the peaches)

Non-stick cooking spray

Step 1:

Preheat the oven to 400 degrees F or 205 degrees C

Step 2:

Take a medium size mixing bowl and add the flour, sugar (not powdered), baking powder, baking soda, and salt. Mix the ingredients and add in the margarine while doing so. The margarine can be difficult to work with so you may want to heat it up in a microwave for 15 seconds, or alternatively cut the margarine into small pieces. Only move onto step 4 when you have a consistent base in the bowl – the margarine should be fully mixed in.

Step 3:

Add the yogurt and the peaches, mixing while you do so.

Step 4:

Take a large piece of wax paper and empty the contents of the bowl onto the paper. Knead the dough for 3-4 minutes. Many are unsure of how to knead the dough, so think about it as folding the dough over itself over and over.

Step 5:

Coat a large baking tray with non-stick spray and form the scones on the tray. The scones look best when shaped like triangles. The exact size of the scones is not as important as making sure the scones are of equal size. This recipe usually yields between 4 and 6 scones. Make sure the dough is firmly pressed against the baking tray. Bake for 12-15 minutes on the center oven rack.

Step 6:

Remove the scones from the oven and while still hot,

paint the scones with milk. This should look like they are slightly moist from the milk. Use this moisture to spread the powdered sugar over the scones. You can serve these right away and they will last about one week at room temperature.

10 Minute Fried Toast – 3 SmartPoints Per Serving

Yes this recipe is truly just a variation of French Toast but I want to stress the importance of a hot breakfast and that it doesn't take too much time to prepare one. This dish can be enjoyed even on a weekday before work and with a little practice you can cut down on the prep time dramatically. This is a dish I commonly make for my daughter before school and it can be made almost as fast as some simple scrambled eggs.

Ready in 10 Minutes

5 minutes to prep and 5 minutes to cook

Ingredients (serves 2):

4 egg whites

6 slices of wheat bread (you'll have lots of options of bread but I suggest looking at the low calorie version. I have switched to 40-45 calorie bread per slice and haven't noticed a big difference. The slices are a little smaller but each piece is less than half the calories of traditional white bread)

¼ cup of 1% milk

2 tablespoons of sugar free maple syrup (this recipe changes to 5 SmartPoints per serving with regular

syrup)

1 tablespoon of cinnamon

1 tablespoon of vanilla extract

Non-stick cooking spray

Step 1:

In a shallow mixing bowl, add the egg whites, milk, and vanilla extract. Whisk these ingredients together.

Step 2:

Coat a skillet with cooking spray and put it over low-medium heat. Dip both sides of your wheat bread into the mixing bowl from step 1 and add to the skillet. You should be able to cook roughly 2 pieces at a time.

Step 3:

While still hot, sprinkle cinnamon on each piece of toast. Serve with syrup and enjoy right away.

3 Minute Breakfast Mug – 2 SmartPoints Per Serving

Perhaps you thought 10 minutes was too long to dedicate to cooking a warm breakfast, well then this recipe is for you. This is a breakfast I used to make at the office as the ingredients can be stored easily in a refrigerator. You will absolutely need to use the liquid egg substitute as opposed to liquid eggs as the substitute will cook better in the microwave. If you have never used your microwave as a primary cooking tool, do not fear – this too was my first recipe cooked entirely in a microwave. When you get a look at the finished product you will be highly satisfied with the result – it tastes great too.

Ready in 3 Minutes

1 minute to prep and 2 minutes to cook

Ingredients (serves 1):

½ cup of liquid egg substitute

1 ounce of low-fat turkey breast (optional)

1 slice of American cheese

Non-stick cooking spray

Step 1:

Take a microwave-safe mug and coat it with the non-stick spray.

Step 2:

Pour the egg substitute into the mug and microwave on high for 1 minute.

Step 3:

Add in the cheese and optionally the turkey. If you're adding the turkey, you will want to make sure that it is in very fine pieces. Microwave for an additional minute.

Saturday Morning Enriching Oatmeal - 7 SmartPoints

This filling breakfast will have you thinking differently about oatmeal. We take a hearty essential oatmeal recipe and add a combination of zesty flavors that make the dish shine. This breakfast takes longer than the others to cook and is best enjoyed on a weekend, or when you have some extra time before starting your day. This recipe can easily be doubled or tripled to serve the entire family.

Ready in 30 Minutes

10 minutes to prep and 20 minutes to cook

Ingredients (serves 1):

½ cup raw oats

2 teaspoons of lemon juice

1/8 teaspoon of cinnamon

1/8 teaspoon of salt

1 low-calorie sweetener packet similar to Splenda

1 cup of unsweetened almond milk, or vanilla soy milk

1 cup of water

Step 1:

In a small pot, combine the oats, cinnamon, salt,

almond milk, and water.

Step 2:

Heat the pot on high heat and bring the oatmeal to a near boil. Once bubbling reduce the heat to low. Cook for 10-15 minutes after the oatmeal has been put to low heat.

Step 3:

Stir occasionally and remove from burner when the oatmeal has thickened.

Step 4:

Before serving, add the sweetener packet to the serving bowl.

LUNCH RECIPES THAT WILL KEEP YOU SATISFIED ALL AFTERNOON

Home Joe's Mediterranean Hummus With Pita Bread – 4 Smart Points Per Serving

This recipe is based on a small love affair I have for the Trader Joe's Mediterranean Hummus. I have tweaked this recipe to get very much the same taste, but with all the added benefit of knowing exactly what ingredients are used. This hummus is packed full of healthy fats from the chick peas, fats that will leave you satisfied all afternoon. I love to bring a small container to work and pair it with either pita chips or pita bread and a side of fresh vegetables – carrots and peppers in particular. Be on the lookout for the nutritional information on the chips or pita bread of your choice – while the hummus is healthy, aim for a serving of less than 200 calories for whatever you choose to dip in the hummus and add 2 smart points to the meal. Feel free to use as many veggies as you want for dipping though, think about these as 0 points.

Ready in 30 Minutes

30 minutes to prepare.

Ingredients (serves 8):

A food processor that can hold 3 cups

1 large garlic glove

2 tablespoons of tahini

½ lemon

6 tablespoons of extra virgin olive oil (the taste is important here, so use extra virgin instead of "pure")

¼ teaspoon of cumin

1 teaspoon of crushed red pepper

½ cup of boiling water

Step 0:

This recipe is dependent on your food processor. You won't need to prepare any ingredients, but make sure that your processor is up to the task. I have had this recipe come out just a tad too lumpy in the past because of the food processor, so blending time may vary slightly to get the consistency that you want.

Step 1:

Put the garlic clove and the processor and pulse 3 to 4 times. Add the rest of the ingredients except for the water.

Step 2:

Run the processor for 3-5 minutes, periodically

switching from pulse to long sustained processing.

Step 3:

Pour in the hot water (does not need to be exactly boiling) and run the processor for an additional 30 seconds to a minute. Check the consistency of the hummus and run the processor for additional time if needed. You may need to add more than ½ a cup of water depending in the consistency of the beans and how powerful your food processor is.

Step 4:

With the desired consistency, pour the hummus in to a container and store in the fridge for several hours. Serving right away will not yield the best flavor as the ingredients are still settling.

Step 5 (Optional):

If serving for a party or if you simply want slightly more indulgent hummus, add a drizzle of olive oil to the hummus before serving.

5 Minute Turkey Wrap – 8 SmartPoints Per Serving

I ate these wraps nearly three times a week for half a year – they were just that delicious. They're easy to make and great to bring as a bagged lunch.

Ready in 5 Minutes

5 minutes to prep and 0 minutes to cook

Ingredients (serves 1)

3 ounces of low-sodium turkey breast (I encourage you to use your local deli counter versus the prepackaged meats – the deli counter meats will often have less sodium so even if you aren't purchasing 'low-sodium' turkey, it is probably still worth it to buy from the deli counter)

1 ounce of lettuce or spinach

¼ of one whole tomato

1 tablespoon of low-fat ranch dressing

1 ounce of low-fat mozzarella cheese (you can use other cheeses, but for the calorie to size ratio, I find mozzarella to be the best investment)

1 wrap or flatbread that is between 100-150 calories per wrap/flatbread (your supermarket will have several options for you but I suggest the Flatout Wraps. These wraps are fluffy and delicious are only

90 calories. For wraps above 150 calories, add another SmartPoint to the recipe)

Step 1:

Take out your wrap or flatbread and heat it in the microwave for 15-20 seconds – this will fluff up your wrap and make it more malleable to shape.

Step 2:

Spread your low-fat ranch dressing over the wrap. Fill the wrap with your turkey, lettuce or spinach, tomatoes, and cheese.

Step 3:

Roll up your wrap and store for lunch or eat right away.

Slow Cooker Southern Style Chicken Soup -4 SmartPoints Per Serving

It's an all day affair that that will last you all week and then some. This hearty soup is great in the winter and full of exotic blends of flavors that will have you wondering why you don't eat soup more often. Since this recipe produces a fairly large batch, it's worth noting that this soup freezes extremely well. If you decide to freeze individual servings, simply let the soup thaw at room temperature before you reheat in the microwave – this is the best way to preserve the flavor.

Ready in 7 Hours

10 minutes to prep and 6-8 hours to cook

Ingredients (serves 10)

2 large chicken breasts cut into inch size cubes

1 clove of finely minced garlic

1 cup of corn (canned is what I use)

½ diced large white onion

½ cup of finely chopped chilantro

1 teaspoon of cumin

1 tablespoon of chili powder

15 ounces of washed and drained kidney beans

(canned is what I use)

15 ounces of washed and drained black beans

(canned is what I use)

1 teaspoon of lime juice

2 whole bell peppers cut into long strips

1 15 ounce can of diced tomatoes

Pepper to taste

Salt to taste

Step 1:

Prepare all of your ingredients and pour them into your slow cooker. Put the slow cookers on low heat and let cook for 6-8 hours. To make sure that the soup is done, reach for a piece of chicken and slice to find the color in the center. Note that it is very difficult to overcook this recipe – even 9 hours in the slow cooker will result in a fantastic soup.

Alternative: If you do not have a slow cooker, do not fret – a regular pot on low heat on your burner will do just fine. There are some limitations however in that you will need to be present the entire time the soup is cooking. It is also possible to overcook the soup if you are using a traditional pot (I first made this recipe using this method and it turned out great. It does require time and patience if you're using a pot, but it can be made over the weekend and enjoyed all week long).

Healthy Zone Calzone – 4 SmartPoints Per Serving

I love this recipe because it uses a neat trick – we substitute heavy dough for Pillsbury and get to cut down on the cooking time in the process. This dish is great by itself and works great as a lunch served at room temperature. If you decide to make the marinara sauce in the next chapter, try it as a dipping sauce for this delicious healthy calzone.

Ready in 40 Minutes

25 minutes to prep and 15 minutes to cook

Ingredients (serves 8):

1 can of reduced fat crescent rolls by Pillsbury (this is absolutely necessary to get the right amount of dough to calorie ratio)

¼ cup of reduce fat shredded cheese (mozzarella is my go to choice but feel free to use your favorite).

6 ounces of low-fat chicken breast

2 cups of baby spinach

6 tablespoons of low-fat whipped cream cheese (you can also use reduced fat but know that it changes the total SmartPoints per serving quite significantly).

1-2 tablespoons of vegetable oil

Step 1:

Take the chicken breast and cut it into cubes before cooking in a frying pan. Use the vegetable oil to cook the chicken and try to use the least amount of oil possible. This recipe is extremely lean and the vegetable oil is actually one of the more calorie expensive ingredients – any savings here do add up.

Step 2:

Preheat the oven to 375 degrees F or 190 degrees C.

Step 3:

Remove the Pillsbury rolls and arrange them on an ungreased baking tray. The container should contain 8 rolls but we are only making 4 calzones. Combine rolls to make the 4 calzones and make sure each roll is flat on the tray.

Step 4:

Spread over each roll the baby spinach, cream cheese, chicken, and your choice of shredded cheese. These rolls are fairly small for how stuffed these calzones will be (definitely a good thing), so you may need to kneed some of the ingredients into the dough itself – this works particularly well with the cream cheese and shredded cheese.

Step 5:

Form each of the individual 4 calzones, fold the dough over the ingredients and 'close' the calzone. This step can be a little tricky if the dough is not at room temperature. The final shape should look a little bit like a crescent moon

Step 6:

Bake for 10-15 minutes in the middle rack of the oven. You will know when the calzones are ready as the dough will begin to flake and turn brown.

8 Minute Tuna – 3 SmartPoints Per Serving

I still prepare this Tuna Salad at least twice a month. It's quick and easy and great to bring to work. If you feel like you're missing out on the pure indulgence of 'fatty' flavors then this salad will hit the spot. Even though we are using low-fat mayonnaise, it still hits all the right notes and you'd be hard pressed to tell the difference between this and a much more calorie dense mayonnaise base. One of the greatest aspects of this recipe, and why it's only 3 SmartPoints per serving, is the use of lettuce as the base for wraps.

We use lettuce for a couple of reasons: one, the neutral flavor of the lettuce brings out the creaminess of the salad without distorting the taste and two, the crispness of the lettuce is essential for the proper texture. I came up with the idea for using lettuce as a base after eating Korean barbeque. Try it and you'll see how it really does bring out the flavor.

Ready in 8 Minutes

8 minutes to prep and 0 minutes to cook

Ingredients (serves 4):

12 ounces of albacore white tuna in water (essential

as this tuna has the meatiest texture and taste)

3 tablespoons of low-fat mayonnaise

3 stalks o chopped celery (if any part of the stalk is not hard, then do not use that section. You want the celery to be firm as to add a crunchiness to the salad).

1 teaspoon of Dijon mustard

½ teaspoon of black pepper

½ teaspoon of table-salt (do not use sea-salt as the harsher grain does not spread as evenly throughout the salad)

½ head of lettuce cut into large pieces (these will serve as the wraps for eating the tuna so keep that in mind as you cut the lettuce)

Step 1:

Drain the tuna and add to a large mixing bowl. Add the celery, pepper, salt, mustard, and mayonnaise. Stir well, breaking up the large pieces of tuna that might be sticking together from the can.

Step 2:

For best results, leave the salad in the fridge for 20 minutes to let thicken. Serve with the large pieces of lettuce.

Week-Long Rice With Chicken – 4 SmartPoints Per Serving

One of the essentials of preparing a good lunch is not having to worry about side dishes. This dish comes with everything you need – protein to keep you full, carbohydrates to give you afternoon energy, and veggies for your general nutrition and to flavor the dish. This rice dish can be stored away for work and can be enjoyed at room temperature or even cold – it will still taste delicious!

Ready in 30 Minutes

15 minutes to prep and 15 minutes to cook

Ingredients (serves 6):

2 large lean, boneless chicken breasts

2 large eggs

2 cups uncooked brown rice

½ cup of pea

½ cup of chopped carrots

2 finely chopped cloves of garlic

2 tablespoons of soy sauce (1 tablespoon if using low-sodium soy sauce – better results are gotten with regular soy)

4 tablespoons of water

Non-stick cooking spray or if unavailable, 1

tablespoon of vegetable oil

Step 1:

Take the chicken breast and cut the chicken into long strips. The important part of cutting the chicken is that each strip has roughly the same thickness. Do not worry about how thick or thin your chicken is – just make sure it is fairy uniform.

Step 2:

Cook the brown rice on your stovetop. Use 5 cups of water for the 2 cups of brown rice. This is more water than is typically used and you will need to cook the rice for slightly longer. The rice will fluff up much more with that extra cup of water. Move onto step 3 only after the rice is done.

Step 3:

In a large skillet, scramble the two large eggs and set aside.

Step 4:

Coat the same skillet again with non-stick cooking spray. Each skillet is a little bit difference and if you know that non-stick spray is not going to be able to grease the entire pan, use 1 tablespoon of vegetable oil, as we do not want the chicken to stick to the pan. Add the sliced chicken and cook halfway before adding the carrots. As the chicken starts to look fully cooked, add the chopped garlic and peas.

Step 4:

Take the soy sauce and pour it into a small dish with the water. Mix and pour into the skillet. The water will evaporate and ensure that the soy sauce is not too overpowering. Move onto step 5 once the chicken is fully cooked and the water is mostly evaporated.

Step 5:

Add into the skillet the cooked rice and scrambled eggs. Mix well and remove from the burner once the eggs have warmed up. Serve right away.

Admiral David's Broccoli - 5 SmartPoints Per Serving

If the name seems familiar, or just a bit off, that's because it is indeed a variation of General Tso's Chicken. It's a standard American Chinese dish that incorporates crisp chicken, spice, and a tinge of orange flavoring. This recipe is derived from a dish a college roommate of mine used to make. If you guessed his name is David, then you would be correct. As with many of the other lunch dishes, this one is also great when served cold. This dish is a complete meal and doubles as a fantastic dinner that is quick to make.

Ready in 25 Minutes

15 minutes to prep and 10 minutes to cook

Ingredients (serves 4):

2 large chicken breasts

1 orange, cut and peeled

1 teaspoon of corn starch

4 teaspoon of vegetable oil

1 bag of precut broccoli florets (should equal roughly 2 cups)

1 tablespoon of minced ginger

¼ cup water (to mix with soy sauce)

3 tablespoons of soy sauce

¼ cup of orange juice

½ cup of chicken or vegetable broth

½ cup water (for help in cooking broccoli)

Step 1:

Take the chicken breasts and cut into long strips. Add the soy sauce to the ¼ cup of water and mix, set aside. During this step, make sure that your other ingredients are all set and ready to go. Once the pan heats up the cooking processes is very fast.

Step 2:

Add the vegetable oil to a large skillet warm over medium heat. Add the chicken strips and cook halfway – add the ginger and continue to cook the chicken until it is entirely done. Take the chicken and ginger out of the skillet and set aside.

Step 3:

Return to the skillet and add the broccoli. You should not need to add any additional oil but if when removing the chicken the pan was left dry, add an additional teaspoon. As the broccoli starts to lightly brown add the ½ cup of water and cover the skillet. Let the broccoli steam for 3 minutes. Check the broccoli to make sure that it is cooked through and not too raw.

Step 4:

Add the cooked chicken and ginger to the skillet. Add the soy sauce mixed with water, the orange juice, and the chicken broth. Mix these ingredients well and allow to cook for an additional 5 minutes. If the chicken or broccoli is beginning to be overcooked, change the heat to low or turn off the burner.

Step 5:

Add in the cornstarch and continue to mix. Once the cornstarch has been mixed in, add the orange peels to the top of the dish and cook for an additional minute or two. Serve right away.

DINNER RECIPES FOR
THE HEALTHY BODY

Lightning Fast Curry Noodles - 3 SmartPoints Per Serving

This is a recipe I commonly refer to when I'm looking to make a quick dinner with just a bit of Asian flair. My favorite aspect to this recipe is that by using rice noodles you do not need to cook the noodles in a pot of boiling water. It can be made with just about any protein, including eggs or tofu. This particular version is vegetarian free, but adding cooked chicken or beef works just as well. This is my own recipe is supposed to mimic Singapore Noodles, a dish commonly found at Chinese restaurants throughout the country.

Ready In 20 Minutes:

10 minutes to prepare and 10 minutes to cook

Ingredients (serves 4)

3 large eggs

2 tablespoons whole milk (or half and half)

3 teaspoons of curry powder

2 tablespoons of vegetable oil

2 whole white mushrooms

1 bell pepper

1 package of Rice Noodles (you will want to go for

medium thickness in the noodle – the particular brand does not matter)

2 tablespoons of soy sauce (low sodium soy sauce will *taste* more salty than regular soy sauce. If using low sodium soy then only use 1 tablespoon)

Step 1:

Take a large bowl or pot and fill it with warm water. The water does not need to approach boiling, and running hot water from your tap will suffice. Once the bowl is full, put the package of rice noodles into the water. You want to check back in a few minutes to make sure that every noodle is submerged in the water.

Step 2:

Slice the mushrooms and bell peppers into small slices. This dish will look a lot like a noodle stir fry, so cut the peppers in long strips and the mushrooms into thin slices.

Step 3:

While the noodles are soaking, use a small frying pan and with the milk and 3 eggs, make scrambled eggs. Once the eggs are made put them aside on a separate plate and cut the scrambled eggs into small pieces.

Step 4:

As the eggs are cooking, take a pan suitable for stir fry and add the vegetable oil. If you do not have a suitable stir fry pan, you can also use a standard pot for boiling pasta. Bring the heat to medium high and once the oil is hot add the mushrooms. As the mushrooms start to cook, add the peppers.

Step 5:

Strain the rice and noodles and add them to the pan with the mushrooms and the bell peppers. Note that the noodles should still appear to be a little bit brittle, do not worry as they will continue to cook in the pan.

Step 6:

As the noodles are cooking in the pan, add the soy sauce and mix thoroughly. Once the sauce is mixed, add the curry powder and stir thoroughly. The noodles should start to take on a dark yellowish color and at this point they should be thoroughly cooked through.

Step 7:

Add the cooked eggs to the pan, and then serve immediately. If the scrambled eggs are slightly cold, they will be warmed up through the cooked noodles.

Step 8:

Serve immediately and enjoy! This meal also works great for lunch. If you are unable to reheat the noodles while at work, they taste great just at room temperature.

Simple Season Chicken- 3 SmartPoints Per Serving

This recipe is a great healthy way to make seasoned chicken cutlets. These cutlets have just the right amount of seasoning and come packed with all the healthy protein of lean chicken breast. This recipe can altered slightly to make a lean type of chicken parmesan. See the altered steps 4 and 5 if you wish to go this route, otherwise this recipe is great with a side of spinach or any other side vegetable.

Ready In 35 Minutes

10 minutes to prepare and 25 minutes to cook

Ingredients (serves 4)

Chicken breast (use roughly 1 pound and cut into 4 large filets)

1/8 teaspoon paprika

¼ cup of parmesan cheese (grated finely)

½ teaspoon of garlic powder

1 teaspoon of parsley (optional)

black pepper to taste

3 tablespoons of dried breadcrumbs

Directions:

Step 1:

Preheat your oven to 400 degrees F or 205 degrees C

Step 2:

Take a small mixing bowl and add the breadcrumbs, grated parmesan, garlic powder, and paprika. Add a pinch of black pepper but know that you can add more while the chicken is cooking.

Step 3:

Take your sliced pieces of chicken breast and dip them into the bowl. Coat both sides of each piece of chicken. Since we are using a healthier version of traditional chicken parmesan, you might have some difficult having the mix stick to the chicken. It is best dip the chicken in the bowl right after you wash the chicken, using the moisture to get it to stick properly.

Step 4:

Prepare a nonstick baking tray and align the pieces of chicken towards the center of the baking tray. Alternate for Chicken Parmesan: Using the Homemade Multi-Purpose Marina sauce (the next recipe in the book), lather the chicken liberally in 2-3 cups of sauce. You will need to use a deeper baking dish to cook the Chicken Parmesan. Once the sauce and chicken has been laid out, coat with shredded Parmesan Cheese and whole slices of mozzarella. To use an appropriate amount of cheese, only layer the cheese on top of the chicken filets. Note that this adds roughly 2 Smart Points to each serving.

Step 5:

Let the chicken bake in the oven for 25 minutes. Check at about 20 minutes as thinner pieces of chicken will cook more quickly. 25 minutes is around the upper limit for how long it will take to cook the chicken.

Alternate for Chicken Parmesan: Using the oven set to 400 degrees F, bake for 35-40 minutes.

Step 6: Remove the chicken form the baking tray and serve within 5-10 minutes.

Homemade Multi-Purpose Marinara – 3 Smart Points Per Serving

This is a great recipe to try out on the weekend and use all week long. Whether it's topping for Chicken Parmesan, dipping sauce for bread, or the foundation of a great pasta dish, this marinara sauce will leave you with plenty of options for how to enjoy it.

Ready in 30 Minutes

10 minutes to prepare and 20 minutes to cook

Ingredients (makes 1 quart)

2 large cloves of garlic

4 large tomatoes

1 28 ounce can of peeled tomatoes

3 tablespoons of olive oil (use extra virgin olive oil – the taste will make a huge difference)

1 ½ tablespoons of sugar

½ teaspoon of ground black pepper

1 teaspoon of salt

½ large white onion

Step 1:

Take your fresh tomatoes and dice them into small chunks. You can also optionally peel the skin from the tomatoes for a smoother sauce. During this step also chop your half onion and your garlic cloves.

Step 2:

In large sauce pan, heat the olive oil under a medium heat, add the diced onion. Wait until the onion is firmly sautéing before adding the garlic.

Step 3:

Add your chopped tomatoes and your can of tomatoes. Also stir in your black pepper and salt. Bring the heat up to medium high and wait for the sauce to boil. Stir frequently and let the sauce boil for 15 minutes.

Step 4:

Turn the heat down to low on the burner and let the sauce simmer for an additional 30 minutes.

Savory Grilled Salmon – 4 Smart Points Per Serving

If there's a common theme with this cookbook, it's the idea that healthy proteins are the foundation to a great diet. Even if you do not normally love salmon, or if you've never tried it, this recipe is certainly worth a shot. At 4 SmartPoints per serving, a side dish of potatoes and spinach will bring the total meal to a reasonable 6-7 SmartPoints, meanwhile the salmon will keep you full until morning.

Ready in 50 Minutes

30 minutes to prep and 20 minutes to cook

Ingredients (serves 4):

1 pound of skinless salmon fillet. You will want the thickness of the salmon to be about 1 inch.

¼ cup of soy sauce

Non-stick cooking spray

1 tablespoon of rice wine vinegar

¼ cup of dry sherry

1 tablespoon of brown sugar

1 teaspoon of garlic powder

1/8 teaspoon of ginger

Black pepper to taste

Step 1:

Preheat the oven to 375 degrees F or 190 degrees C. Make sure the grill rack is in the center of the oven.

Step 2:

Combine the sherry, soy sauce, brown sugar, vinegar, garlic powder, and ginger in a mixing bowl.

Step 3:

Dip the filets of salmon in the mixing bowl and place in the refrigerator for 20 minutes to marinade.

Step 4:

Place the remaining marinade in a small saucepan and heat on low. The marinade will begin to thicken as the salmon marinades in the refrigerator.

Step 5:

Spray the grill rack with non-stick spray and place the salmon filets on the rack. The cooking time for the salmon will differ greatly depending on thickness. As a guideline each side will need 4 to 8 minutes to cook through. The sign that the salmon is fully cooked is when it begins to flake.

Step 6:

Remove the salmon from the oven and place it on a large serving plate. Coat the salmon in the remaining marinade. Serve immediately.

Cheesy Baked Chicken – 5 SmartPoints Per Serving

I love this dish if for no other reason than it remind me that dieting does not need to omit cream and cheese. This chicken dish has all the flavor of a delicious casserole without any of the guilt. A simple side dish like a lightly tossed salad goes great, just be sure not to overdo it with the dressing.

Ready in 55 minutes:

10 minutes to prep and 45 minutes to cook

Ingredients (serves 8):

2 cups of cooked macaroni noodles

2 cups of 1% fat skin milk

2 cups of chopped boneless chicken breasts cut into cubes

8 ounces of low-fat shredded cheddar cheese

2 cups of undiluted cream of mushroom soup (I personally use Campbell's brand)

Step 1:

Preheat the oven to 350 degrees F or 175 degrees C.

Step 2:

Use a baking dish that is 2 inches deep, similar to a casserole dish, and place the cream of mushroom soup, the skim milk, cooked macaroni, shredded cheese, and uncooked chicken breasts into the baking tray. Mix thoroughly.

Step 3:

Place the baking tray in the center oven rack and bake for 35 minutes. At 35 minutes, take the baking tray out of the oven and remove a piece of chicken. Cut the chicken in half to see if it is cooked all the way through. Typically this recipe calls for 45 minutes, but if the chicken pieces are small enough the dish could be done in 35. Cook for an additional 10 minutes if needed.

Step 4:

45 minutes is the upper limit for cooking the casserole, but always make sure to slice the chicken and make sure that it is cooked all the way through. Small variables could mean cooking for an additional 5-10 minutes.

Step 5:

Let the dish cook for 10 minutes before serving.

Lean Mean Pork Chops - 3 SmartPoints Per Serving

In this recipe we are using our oven to bypass the unnecessary oil we'd get in by using a frying pan. This will lead to a more brazen pork that should be more tender. This dish takes longer than several of our other dinners and so use this time to experiment with side dishes. A vegetable melody goes great as the extra time gives you the opportunity to wash and cut your vegetables. You can also use the already heated oven for simple sliced baked potatoes - even the spices from the pork can be reused if you wish.

Ready in 70 Minutes

20 minutes to prep and 50 minutes to cook

Ingredients Needed (serves 4):

Non-stick cooking spray

1 large egg white

¼ teaspoon of ground ginger

1/8 teaspoon of garlic powder

2 tablespoon of pineapple juice

6 ounces of pork loin (try and get lean pork if available)

1 tablespoon of soy sauce

¼ teaspoon of paprika

1/3 cup dried breadcrumbs

¼ teaspoon of dried Italian seasoning

Step 1:

Preheat the oven to 350 degrees F or 175 degrees C

Step 2:

If you were able to purchase lean pork loin then you do not need to follow this step. If you were not able to purchase lean pork loin, trim away as much fat as you can. Do not worry about the taste – our seasoning will make up for the flavor.

Step 3:

In large mixing bowl, add the soy sauce, garlic powder, egg white, ginger, and pineapple juice. Mix well as the egg white is sometimes difficult to mix thoroughly.

Step 4:

Using a separate bowl, mix breadcrumbs, Italian seasoning, and the paprika.

Step 5:

Take the pork chops and dip them into the wet mixing bowl and then dip them into the dry mixing bowl. Coat the pork chops well but know that some ingredients will be left.

Step 6:

Lay the pork chops on the baking tray. Bake for 25-30 minutes on each side. Wait 3-5 minutes before serving.

Fast Cooking Scallops - 3 SmartPoints Per Serving

The hardest part of this recipe is the trip to the supermarket to purchase scallops. Do not fear as frozen scallops will work just fine, and if you are inexperienced cooking fish you also do not have to worry - this recipe is built upon the idea that perhaps this is your first time cooking fish in a pan. If you are unsure about whether to try this recipe, think about scallops as the 'meatier' shrimp. For a side dish, I recommend a baked potato and spinach or zucchini. The lemon goes great with subtle side dishes like these.

Ready in 20 Minutes

10 minutes to prep and 10 minutes to cook

Ingredients (serves 4):

1 pound of sea scallops, dried

2 tablespoons of all purpose flour

1 tablespoon of virgin olive oil

1 tablespoon of lemon juice

1 minced scallions

¼ teaspoon of salt

2 tablespoons of parsley

Pinch of sage (nice flavor, but not necessary if you don't already have this spice)

Step 1:

Take a mixing bowl and add the flour, scallions, and salt.

Step 2:

Take the scallops and dip them in the mixing bowl. Don't worry about how much of the mix ends up on the scallions – it should only be a small layer and does not necessary need to cover the scallops entirely.

Step 3:

Take a large skillet and heat the olive oil under medium heat. Toss the scallops one at a time into the pan. The scallops should could in about 4 minutes. Be careful not to overcook the scallops as they will become very though. You will know the scallops are done when they become impossible to see through the skin.

Step 4:

If the scallops were made in batches, add all of the scallops back into the pan, turning off the heat before you do so. Add the chopped parsley and lemon juice. Mix well and serve right away

About The Author

Hi there it's Diana here, I want to share a little bit about myself so that we can get to know each other on a deeper level. I grew up in California and have lived there for the better part of my life. Being exposed to many different cultures, people, and food, those experiences have certainly influenced my style of cooking and shaped my perception of the world in many profound ways. Cooking has always been a passion of mine since I was young and I made it a goal to one day become a master chef, bringing food to people that are one-of-a-kind. Fast forward a few decades and I have succeeded in my dreams which I am extremely grateful and proud of. With my husband and two kids, I now live a very happy and fulfilled life. One I wouldn't trade anything in the world for.

CPSIA information can be obtained
at www.ICGtesting.com
Printed in the USA
LVHW022120051120
670845LV00014B/1843